FAUNA OF MANITOBA

MAMMALS AND BIRDS

By
ERNEST THOMPSON SETON

British Library Cataloguing-in-Publication Data

A catalogue record for this book is available from the
British Library

Ernest Thompson Seton

Ernest Thompson Seton was born on 14th August 1860, in South Shields, County Durham, England. He grew up to be a pioneering author, wildlife artist, founder of the Woodcraft Indians, and one of the originators of the Boy Scouts of America (BSA).

The Seton family emigrated to Canada when Ernest was just six years old, and most of his childhood was consequently spent in Toronto. As a youth, he retreated to the woods to draw and study animals as a way of avoiding his abusive father – a practice which shaped the rest of his adult life. On his twenty-first birthday, Seton's father presented him with a bill for all the expenses connected with his childhood and youth, including the fee charged by the doctor who delivered him. He paid the bill, but never spoke to his father again.

Originally known as Ernest Evan Thompson, Ernest changed his name to Ernest Thompson Seton, believing that Seton had been an important name in his paternal line. He became successful as a writer, artist and naturalist, and moved to New York City to further his career. Seton later lived at 'Wyndygoul', an estate that he built in Cos Cob, a section of Greenwich, Connecticut. After experiencing vandalism by some local youths, Seton invited the young miscreants to his estate for a weekend, where he told them what he claimed were stories of the American Indians and of nature.

After this experience, he formed the Woodcraft Indians (an American youth programme) in 1902 and invited the local youth to join (at first just boys, but later girls as well). The stories that Seton told became a series of articles written for the *Ladies Home Journal*, and were eventually collected in *The Birch Bark Roll of the Woodcraft Indians* in 1906. Seton also met Scouting's founder, Lord Baden-Powell, in 1906. Baden-Powell had read Seton's book of stories, and was greatly intrigued by it. After the pair had met and shared ideas, Baden-Powell went on to found the Scouting movement worldwide, and Seton became vital in the foundation of the Boy Scouts of America (BSA) and was its first Chief Scout (from 1910 – 1915). Despite this large achievement, Seton quickly became embroiled in disputes with the BSA's other founders, Daniel Carter Beard and James E. West.

In addition to disputes about the content of Seton's contributions to the Boy Scout Handbook, conflicts also arose about the suffrage activities of his wife, Grace, and his British citizenship (it being *an American* organization). In his personal life, Seton was married twice. The first time was to Grace Gallatin in 1896, with whom he had one daughter, Ann (who later changed her name to Anya), and secondly to Julia M. Buttree, with whom he adopted an infant daughter, Beulah (who also changed her first name, to Dee). Alongside his work with the Woodcraft Indians and the BSA, Seton also found time to pursue his primary interest – that of nature writing.

Seton was an early pioneer of animal fiction writing, his most popular work being *Wild Animals I Have Known* (1898), which contains the story of his killing of the wolf Lobo. He later became involved in a literary debate known as the nature fakers controversy, after John Burroughs published an article in 1903 in the *Atlantic Monthly* attacking writers of sentimental animal stories. The controversy lasted for four years and included important

American environmental and political figures of the day, including President Theodore Roosevelt. Seton was also associated with the Santa Fe arts and literary community during the mid-1930s and early 1940s, which comprised a group of artists and authors including author and artist Alfred Morang, sculptor and potter Clem Hull, painter Georgia O'Keeffe, painter Randall Davey, painter Raymond Jonson, leader of the Transcendental Painters Group, and artist Eliseo Rodriguez.

In 1931, Seton became a United States citizen. He died on 23rd October, 1946 (aged eighty-six) in Seton Village in northern New Mexico. Seton was cremated in Albuquerque. In 1960, in honour of his 100th birthday and the 350th anniversary of Santa Fe, his daughter Dee and his grandson, Seton Cottier (son of Anya), in a fitting tribute to the man who loved his surrounding countryside so much, scattered his ashes over Seton Village from an airplane.

FAUNA OF MANITOBA

(Mammals and Birds)

By ERNEST THOMPSON SETON,

Naturalist to the Government of Manitoba.

MANITOBA is 268 by 252 miles, or 74,448 square miles. It lies wholly within the great wheat belt of the north-west, but faunally speaking it is in the Temperate Region, partly in the Canadian Life-zone and partly in the Alleghanian portion of the Transition Zone. A line drawn from the south-east corner to the north-west corner would nearly demark these two zones. The *Canadian area*, north-east of this line, is nearly all forested. The prevailing trees being black spruce, white spruce and jack pine. The *Alleghanian area*, south-west of the line, comprises the prairies of the Province, and a considerable region of aspen forest.

Riding, Duck and Porcupine Mountains may be considered Canadian islands in the Alleghanian region.

MAMMALS OF MANITOBA

(The nomenclature is that of the United States Biological Survey.)

1. **Wapiti or Canadian Elk,** *Cervus canadensis* Erxleben. Formerly found in all the Alleghanian region of the Province. Reduced to a few stragglers twenty years ago, but since then, owing to good game laws, they have speedily increased and now furnish a regular supply of game. The estimated number of Wapiti in Manitoba to-day is 5,000.

2. **Northern White-tailed Deer,** *Odocoileus virginianus borealis* Miller. Unknown in the Province until

about thirty years ago, since .en it has greatly increased, following the settlers; now found wherever there are settlements adjoining woods.

3. **Mule-deer,** *Odocoileus hemionus* (Rafinesque). Formerly abundant in all the Alleghanian Region; greatly reduced some twenty years ago, but now once more abundant in its proper region, wherever there is cover combined with broken ground

4. **Moose,** *Alces americanus* Jardine. Abundant in all the forested area of the Province; apparently in no danger of extinction, since reasonable game laws have come in force. Several thousand are killed each ear in the Province. The estimated total head of Moose within our limits is between 20,000 and 30,000.

5. **Woodland Caribou,** *Rangifer caribou* (Gmelin). Found only in the Canadian region, and nowhere common. It is more or less migratory, coming fifty to one hundred miles farther south for the winter.

6. **Prong-horned Antelope,** *Antilocapra americana* (Ord). Formerly found in all the prairies of the south-west. Recorded once or twice in early days very near Winnipeg; last seen on the Souris about 1881. Now extinct in the Province.

7. **American Bison or Buffalo,** *Bison bison* (Linnaeus). Formerly found in great abundance on all the prairies of Manitoba. Last seen wild near Winnipeg in 1819. Last great wil* *:d on the Souris 1867; the last wild individual on the Souris 1883.

8. **Red-squirrel,** *Sciuus hudsonicus* Erxleben. Abundant in every timbered portion of Manitoba, and active the year round.

9. **Eastern Chipmunk,** *Tamias striatus griseus* Mearns. Abundant in the woods of the south-eastern part of

the country and westward to Portage la Prairie. Hibernating during the winter.

10. **Little Chipmunk,** *Eutamias quadrivittatus neglectus* (Allen). Of general distribution in the southern half of the Province wherever there is timber and dry land. Exceedingly abu lant, living like the preceding. Hibernating all 'nter.

11. **Franklin Ground-squirrel,** *Citadus franklini* (Sabine Abundant in all the Alleghanian Region of Ma toba wherever there is woodland alternating with open sunny places. Like the rest of the Ground-squirrels it is quite omnivorous, but stores up only vegetable substances for bad weather supplies. It hibernates for six months of each year.

12. **Richardson Ground-squirrel,** *Citellus richardsoni* (Sabine). Exceedingly abundant on all the dry rolling prairies west of Pembina Mountain and south of Lake Manitoba extending up a little way in the Gilbert Plains country and the Upper Assiniboine. Hibernating all winter.

13. **Striped Ground-squirrel** *Citellus 'ridecemlineatus* (Mitchill). Common on all the ⟨ airies of Manitoba, but much less so than in primitive times. Its burrow is so easily disturbed by the plow that cultivation is bound to exterminate it. It hibernates for six months of each year.

14. **Woodchuck,** *Marmota monax canadensis* (Erxleben). Found in all parts of the Province where there is dry woods, but nowhere abundant. More common probably about Duck Mountain than elsewhere. It hibernates for four or five months of the year.

15. **Canadian Flying-squirrel,** *Sciuropterus sabrinus* (Shaw). Common in all parts of the country. Some years very abundant, but rarely seen on account of its nocturnal habits. It is active all winter.

16. **Canada Beaver,** *Castor canadensis* Kuhl.   Formerly
very abundant in all parts of Manitoba.   Reduced
to very few some years ago, but owing to fostering
laws it has since increased and may once more
become plentiful.

17. **Common House-mouse,** *Mus musculus* Linnaeus.
Introduced with settlers in 1882; now abundant in
all towns.

18. **Grasshopper-mouse,** *Onychomys leucogaster* (Wied).
Found only on the dry prairies at the extreme
south-western corner of the Province.

19. **Arctic Deermouse,** *Peromyscus maniculatus arcticus*
(Mearns).   Abundant throughout the country
wherever there is woods; especially fond of frequenting barns and outbuildings that are near the
edge of the forest.   Closely related to it, probably
mere races, are the Prairie Deermouse (*bairdi*)
found in the prairie regions and the plains, or Ne-
braska Deermouse (*nebrascensis*) found in the
Souris country.   True *maniculatus* should be found
in western Manitoba.

20. **Red-backed Vole,** *Evotomys gapperi* (Vigors).   Generally distributed throughout the Province, though
nowhere abundant.   It appears in two races, the
bright colored, large prairie race (*loringi*) and the
small dark race of the Canadian woods (*gapperi*).

21. **Drummond Vole,** *Microtus pennsylvanicus drum-
mondi* (Audubon and Bachman).   Abundant in all
sedgy regions of the Province.   A harmless species
when not in excessive numbers, confining itself to
lowlands overgrown with tall grass.

22. **Little Vole,** *Microtus minor* (Merriam).   Generally
distributed in the south-west or Alleghanian region,
but nowhere very abundant.

23. **Muskrat,** *Fiber zibethicus* (Linnaeus). Found in great numbers wherever there is water throughout the Province. This animal is an important fur-bearer. Two million of its skins are shipped to London every year by the Hudson's Bay Company, representing of course the entire north-west. It lives in the water, and is rarely seen away from it except when forced to migrate.

24. **Northern Bog-lemming,** *Synaptomys borealis* (Richardson). Never actually taken in the Province, but recorded from surrounding localities which justify its inclusion. It is abundant in the far north, but not elsewhere common.

25. **Gray Pocket-gopher,** *Thomomys talpoides* (Richardson). Abundant on the high, dry prairies of Manitoba, but not extending very far into the woods. It is commonly called Mole by the residents, as it forced up mounds of earth in the fashion of the Mole. It is, however, a herbivorous rodent.

26. **Jumping-mouse,** *Zapus hudsonius* (Zimmermann). This extraordinary creature, famous for its long tail and its jumping habits, is found throughout Manitoba, except on the bare prairies. It appears in two forms. The typical Hudsonian, found in the Canadian forest, and the prairie form (*campestris*), a bright colored race peculiar to the woodland edges in the prairie portions of the south-west.

27. **Canada Porcupine,** *Erethizon dorsatum* (Linnaeus). Generally distributed in the Canadian area of Manitoba, but nowhere abundant. Its quills were formerly the favorite material for embroidery among the Indians, but in recent times the squaws have used glass beads in preference, so that the art is dying out.

28. **Snowshoe-hare** or **White-rabbit,** *Lepus americanus phaeonotus* Allen. Found in all parts of Manitoba wherever there is cover. In summer it is brown, in winter pure white. In Turtle Mountain it is repre-sented by the race *bishopi*, distinguished by its short ears and pale color. The prevailing form in Mani-toba is the dusky backed race (*phaeonotus*). This hare has long been noted for the excessive fluctua-tion of its numbers in cycles of seven to ten years. One hundred or more may be seen every day when its numbers are at its height, but usually the plague breaks out at this time and speedily reduces the Snowshoe population to near zero.

29. **Prairie-hare,** *Lepus campestris* Bachman. For-merly found only in the extreme south-west of the Province, and exceedingly rare; now abundant in all the prairie regions, especially in the vicinity of cultivated fields.

30. **Canada Lynx,** *Lynx canadensis* Kerr. Found in all the wooded parts of the Province, but varying greatly in numbers on different years.

31. **Kit-fox or Swift,** *Vulpes velox* (Say). Formerly common on the high dry prairie of the south-west; now exterminated within or : limits.

32. **Royal Fox,** *Vulpes regalis* . *..erriam. Common on the prairies of the province; probably replaced in the woods by the form called *fulvus*. Less nu-merous than formerly.

33. **Gray-wolf or Buffalo-wolf,** *Canis occidentali:* Rich-ardson. Generally distributed, but nowhere com-mon.

34. **Prairie-wolf or Coyote,** *Canis latrans* Say. Abun-dant in all the south-western half of Manitoba; probably as numerous now as in the days before settlement.

35. **Canada Otter,** *Lutra canadensis* (Schreber). Found all along the rivers, but exceedingly rare now.

36. **Bonaparte Weasel,** *Putorius cicognanii* (Bonaparte). Common in most parts of the Province, but varying greatly in numbers on different years.

37. **Least Weasel,** *Putorius rixosus* Bangs. Nowhere numerous, but ranging over the whole Province. This is the smallest known beast of prey.

38. **Long-tailed Weasel,** *Putorius longicauda* (Bonaparte). Abundant in all the prairie region of Manitoba, etc.

39. **Mink,** *Putorius vison* (Schreber). Abundant throughout the Province wherever there is water and swamp.

40. **Spruce Marten,** *Mustela americana abieticola* Preble. Found only in the coniferous forest, and rare there.

41. **Pekan or Fisher,** *Mustela pennanti* Erxleben. Found only in the coniferous forest, and rare.

42. **Wolverene,** *Gulo luscus* (Linnaeus). Rare everywhere, but found in most of the heavily timbered parts of North-eastern Manitoba.

43. **Prairie Skunk,** *Mephitis hudsonica* Richardson. This large Skunk is abundant, especially in the half-wooded region.

44. **Common Badger,** *Taxidea taxus* (Schreber). Common in all prairie region, but not found in the woods; it is less common than before settlement.

45. **Raccoon,** *Procyon lotor* (Linnaeus). Very rare and confined to the south-western part of the Province, along rivers whose banks are heavily wooded.

46. **Grizzly-bear,** *Ursus horribilis* Ord. Now extinct in Manitoba, for perhaps 100 years. The records

show that at one time there were Grizzlies in all the Pembina Hills, Brandon Hills and Turtle Mountain regions.

47. **Black-bear,** *Ursus americanus* Pallas. Quite common yet in all parts of Manitoba where there is cover. Both black and brown phases occur in the same litter.

48. **Cooper Shrew,** *Sorex personatus* I. Geoffroy St. Hilaire. Generally distributed, and very abundant in some seasons.

49. **Richardson Shrew,** *Sorex richardsoni* Bachman. Apparently of general distribution, but not common I have records from Carberry, Shoal Lake, Norway House, etc.

50. **Hoy Shrew,** *Microsorex hoyi* (Baird). All of Manitoba falls within the known range of this species. Yet there is but one actual record, that from Red River Settlement.

51. **Marsh-shrew,** *Neosorex palustris* (Richardson). All Manitoba falls within its known range. but there are only two or three records. It is an inhabitant of marshes and river banks, nowhere common.

52. **Mole-shrew,** *Blarina brevicauda* (Say). Found only in the woods east of Winnipeg; common there.

53. **Star-nosed Mole,** *Condylura cristata* (Linnaeus). Recorded once from Winnipeg, but rare, and near the west end of its range at this point.

54. **Little Brown-bat,** *Myotis lucifugus* (Le Conte). All Manitoba falls within its known range. But I know of but one specimen taken within our limits; that I got from Poplar Point.

55. **Say Bat,** *Myotis subulatus* (Say). The accredited range of this Bat includes Manitoba, and the re-

cords nearly surround the Pro·.: ce, but it has not yet been taken in our limits.

56. **Silver-haired Bat,** *Lasionycteris noctivagans* (Le Conte). This species is commonly and generally distributed in Manitoba. It comes from the south about the vernal, and retires about the autumnal equinox.

57. **Big Brown-bat,** *Eptesicus fuscus* (Beauvois). There is a single Lake Winnipeg record for this species. Its proper range is to the southward, and Manitoba is its northmost limit so far as known.

58. **Red-bat,** *Lasiurus borealis* (Muller). The reco ds show that this handsome bat is found in all the south-western part of the Province as a summer visitant.

59. **Hoary-bat,** *Lasiurus cinereus* (Beauvois). This fine species is found in all parts of Manitoba. It is somewhat common, and, like the rest of our Bats, is a migrant, never, so far as known, hibernating within our limits.

THE BIRDS OF MANITOBA

(The nomenclature used is that of the A.O.U. latest check list)

1. **Swan-grebe, Western Grebe.** *Aechmophorus occi dentalis.* Common summer resident in parts of th Alleghanian region, chiefly towards the north. Quite common at Shoal Lake, near Lake Manitoba, breeding in colonies in the marshes about Lake Winnepegosis. Very local in distribution.

2. **Silver-cheeked Grebe, Holbœll Grebe.** *Colymbus holboelli.* Summer resident in Red River Valley.

Breeding in most of the large marshes of the Alleghanian portion of Manitoba.

3. **Horned Grebe.** *Coiymbus auritus.* Abundant summer resident throughout the Province, April to October.

4. **American Eared-grebe.** *Colymbus nigricollis californicus.* A common summer resident in all the prairie region, but not yet found in the Canadian or north-eastern half of the Province.

5. **Pied-billed Grebe, Dabchick.** *Podilymbus podiceps.* Common summer resident in all parts of the Province where there are small ponds, from mid-April to October.

6. **Loon.** *Gavia immer.* Common summer resident on all the large lakes and rivers that are well supplied with fish.

7. **Red-throated Loon.** *Gavia stellata.* Rare; known only as a migrant.

8. **Long-tailed Skua.** *Stercorarius longicaudus.* In September, 1896, Samuel Slater brought to Alexander Calder of Winnipeg, in whose collection it now is, an immature Long-tailed Skua, shot on Lake Winnipeg. Its dimensions are: Length, $16\frac{1}{2}$ inches; wing 12 inches; tail $6\frac{1}{2}$ inches; tarsus, $1\frac{3}{4}$ inches; middle toe and claw, $1\frac{3}{4}$ inches. All above sooty, except the neck, which is cream color, and crown, which is sharply blackish.

9. **American Herring-gull.** *Larus argentatus.* Abundant; of general distribution. Breeding in all the large lakes and prairie ponds. Arrives April 20.

10. **Ring-billed Gull.** *Larus delawarensis.* Common summer resident. Breeding in all the lakes and large prairie ponds.

11. **Franklin Gull, Rosy Gull.** *Larus franklini.* Abun-

dant; common summer resident, breeding in most of the large marshes of the Alleghanian region.

12. **Bonaparte Gull.** *Larus philadelphia.* Regular summer visitant. A few breed on the large lakes of the Province region.

13. **Forster Tern.** *Sterna forsteri.* Common summer resident, breeding about the larger lakes.

14. **Common Tern.** *Sterna hirundo.* Common summer resident on the large lakes, breeding with the preceding.

15. **Black Tern.** *Hydrochelidon nigra surinamensis.* Abundant summer resident everywhere, breeding in colonies on the prairie ponds. Arrives May 20; departs August 30.

16. **Double-crested Cormorant, Crow-duck.** *Phalacrocorax auritus.* Generally distributed, and breeding in colonies about the large lakes of the Alleghanian part of the country.

17. **American White Pelican.** *Pelecanus erythrorhynchos.* Apparently of general distribution, breeding about most of the lakes, chiefly west of Lake Winnipeg: less numerous than formerly.

18. **American Merganser, Sheldrake.** *Mergus americanus.* Common summer resident, breeding commonly in the rivers of the Lake Winnipegosis basin.

19. **Red-breasted Merganser, Fish-duck.** *Mergus serrator.* Common summer resident. Generally distributed, but breeding only in the northernly parts of the Province.

20. **Hooded Merganser.** *Lophodytes cucullatus.* Common summer resident of general distribution,

breeding wherever it finds hollow trees near the water.

21. **Mallard.** *Anas platyrhynhos.* Very abundant summer resident everywhere, breeding in all marshes. Arrives April 15; departs late in October.

22. **Black Mallard or Dusky Duck.** *Anas rubripes.* Very rare. Three or four specimens taken at Long Lake in four years. In my collection is a specimen from Shoal Lake, taken by Geo. H. Measham in 1901, and another taken near Winnipeg, by W. R. Hine. According to Measham, two more were shot at Shoal Lake in 1899. C. C. Helliwell reports one taken on Lake Manitoba in the fall of 1898.

23. **Gadwall.** *Chaulelasmus streperus.* Common, breeding about all the large lakes and the ponds of the prairie region.

24. **Baldpate or Widgeon.** *Mareca americana.* Summer resident. Not common, but generally distributed and breeding.

25. **Green-winged Teal.** *Nettion carolinense.* Abundant summer resident everywhere; breeding. Arrives April 20; departs in October.

26. **Blue-winged Teal.** *Querquedula discors.* Very abundant summer resident. Arrives late in April; departs early in October.

27. **Shoveller.** *Spatula clypeata.* Common summer resident everywhere. Departs late in October, like the other Ducks, when the frost seals the ponds.

28. **Pintail.** *Dafila acuta.* Common summer resident, breeding. Arrives late in mid-April; departs in October.

29. **Wood-duck.** *Aix sponsa.* A rare but regular summer visitant as far north as Lakes Winnipeg and Winnipegosis. I saw a pair taken at Carberry in 1883, and in 1886 got a male at Kenora. It is reported from Cook's Creek, Westbourne, Portage la Prairie, Lake Winnipegosis. Over a dozen were taken on the Souris River, about 25 miles southwest of Brandon, between 1882 and 1899, by H. W. O. Boger. Three were killed at Brandon by C. C. Helliwell, who saw also two on the roof of the town station, one day about 1890. G. H. Measham reports it rare at Shoal Lake, but one or two are seen there each year.

These, with previous records, completely spot the map of south-western Manitoba. The species is doubtless found throughout the Alleghanian region of the Province, as it has been recorded from Qu'Appelle and Cumberland House.

30. **Redhead.** *Marila americana* Abundant summer resident of the Alleghanian region. Arrives in April; departs in October.

31 **Canvas-back.** *Marila vallisneria.* Generally distributed in the Alleghanian region and breeding, but nowhere common.

32. **American Scaup-duck, Big Blue-bill.** *Marila marila.* Common in spring and fall in all parts of Manitoba; a few may breed in the northern district. Arrives late in April; departs in October.

33. **Lesser Scaup-duck, Little Blue-bill.** *Marila affinis.* Very abundant summer resident in all parts of the Province. Breeds.

34. **Ring-necked Duck, Marsh Blue-bill.** *Marila collaris.* A rare summer resident. Reported from Winnipeg, Portage la Prairie, Waterhen River.

35. **American Golden-eye, Whistler.** *Clangula americana.* A common summer resident in all parts of Manitoba where there are large trees near water.

36. **Barrow Golden-eye.** *Clangula islandica.* "I shot a brace at Lake Manitoba in 1879, and a drake at Shoal Lake in the spring of the following year. And I saw a drake which was killed at the mouth of the Red River." (*R. H. Hunter.*) .

37. **Bufflehead.** *Charitonetta albeola.* Common summer resident wherein there is timber and water. Arrives April 15; departs in October.

38. **White-winged Scoter.** *Oidemia deglandi.* Summer resident, breeding in marshy ponds. Found it quite common at Shoal Lake.

39. **Surf Scoter.** *Oidemia perspicillata.* Rare migrant; reported from Lake Winnipeg (*Hine*), Red River (*Hunter*), Nelson River (*Blakiston*).

40. **Ruddy Duck.** *Erismatura Jamaicensis.* A summer visitant; not common, erratic in distribution. Breeds in most of the large marshes.

41. **Blue Goose, Silver Brant.** *Chen caerulescens.* Noted as a rare migrant. Specimens taken at Winnipeg, Portage la Prairie and Brandon. At Fort Chipewyan, Lake Athabaska, where 10,000 or more geese were killed each autumn, only one of this species was taken in several years. This is now in my. collection.

42. **Snow-goose, Wavey.** *Chen hyperborea.* Abundant spring migrant; less common in the fall. Arrives May 15, and again in October.

43. **Ross Goose.** *Chen rossi.* A specimen was taken on Red River near Winnipeg by Frank Marwood of that city, Sept. 20, 1902. It is now in the collection of Alexander Calder at Winnipeg.

44. **White-fronted Goose.** *Anser albifrons gambeli.* Rare, but regular migrant.

45. **Canada Goose, Wild Goose.** *Branta canadensis.* Abundant in the migrations. Arrives in April; departs late in October.

45. **Hutchins Goose.** *Branta canadensis hutchinsi.* A rare migrant or straggler. Taken on Red River by Kennicott, observed at Portage la Prairie by C. W. Nash, and noted at Brandon by C. C. Helliwell.

46. **Brant.** *Branta bernicla glaucogastra.* A rare migrant.

47. **Whistling Swan.** *Olor columbianus.* A rare migrant of general distribution.

48. **Trumpeter Swan.** *Olor buccinator.* A very rare migrant. George H. Measham secured three on Roseau River. A single specimen is in Manitoba Museum.

49. **American Bittern.** *Botaurus lentiginosus.* Common summer resident; of general distribution, especially about the extensive marshes of the Alleghanian region. Arrives the middle of April; departs in October.

50. **Least Bittern.** *Ixobrychus exilis.* Very rare summer visitant. On Nov. 9, 1907, E. W. Darbey showed me a Least Bittern, a young male, that was taken about Oct. 20 at Oak Point, Lake Manitoba, by J. C. McNab.

  According to W. R. Hine, a specimen was shot in the Bishop's Marsh near St. Boniface in 1885 by Wm. Gordon (of Winnipeg). C. C. Helliwell has seen one or two about Oak Lake, Manitoba. Frank M. Chapman saw one at Shoal Lake, June, 1901.

51. **Great Blue Heron.** *Ardea herodias.* Generally distributed as a summer resident; nowhere common.

52. **American Egret.** *Herodias egretta.* In the summer of 1888, David Armit, an officer of the Hudson's Bay Company stationed at Manitoba House, while out shooting at Duck Bay, Lake Winnipegosis, came across and collected a fine adult specimen of this bird in breeding plumage. He has most generously sent the prize to me; it is now No. 1,776 of my collection. This is, I believe, the northernmost record for the species.

53. **Black-crowned Night-heron.** *Nycticorax nycticorax naevius.* Summer resident of general distribution in the Alleghanian region. I found it quite numerous and breeding in colonies at Shoal Lake. In other parts of the region it is somewhat rare.

54. **Whooping Crane.** *Grus americana.* Formerly common and breeding; now nearly extinct.

55. **Little Brown Crane.** *Grus canadensis.* Summer resident of general distribution; much less common than formerly. Arrives in mid-April; departs in September.

56. **Virginia Rail.** *Rallus virginianus.* Rare, but regular, summer resident of the Alleghanian region. The specimen in my collection was taken near Morden by D. Nicholson. I saw another in the collection of Geo. F. Atkinson of Portage la Prairie, and heard of another at Brandon. I have seen several taken near Winnipeg.

57. **Sora, Common Rail.** *Porzana carolina.* Abundant summer resident throughout Manitoba. Arrives May 1; departs in October.

58. **Yellow Rail, Water Sparrow.** *Coturnicops noveboracensis.* On the 13th of July, 1883, a specimen of this Rail was brought to me alive, by a farmer who caught it in a slough where he was cutting wild hay.

Being just then called away, I placed the bird in a coop, and on my return it was gone. But the record is, I believe, safe, as Preble found the species numerous at York factory, and there are other records to completely surround the Province.

59. **American Coot.** *Fulica americana.* Abundant summer resident. Arrives in mid-April; departs late in October.

60. **Northern Phalarope.** *Lobipes lobatus.* Rare straggler in migration; noted about Winnipeg only.

61. **Wilson Phalarope.** *Steganopus tricolor.* Common summer resident, breeding on most of the large ponds and marshes in the Alleghanian region.

62. **American Avocet.** *Recurvirostra americana.* While abundant in the adjoining Province of Saskatchewan, the species is a rare straggler in Manitoba.
R. H. Hunter writes: "I have killed the bird along the Souris, south-west of Plum Creek." In the Museum of the Geological Survey at Ottawa is a specimen of the Avocet, marked "from Manitoba." Shaw Cottingham killed nearly a dozen at a place 9 miles south of Brandon in 1899, and C. C. Helliwell got three or four out of a flock at Oak Lake, ten years before.

63. **American Woodcock.** *Philohela minor.* Very rare summer resident. At Winnipeg W. R. Hine reports that he got four during four years. At Portage la Prairie, one or two pairs seen each year by C. W. Nash. At Stuartburn, on Roseau River, George H. Measham shot one in 1891.

64. **Wilson Snipe.** *Gallinago delitcata.* Abundant summer resident on all extensive bogs. Arrives April 20; departs September 30.

65. **Dowitcher.** *Macrorhamphus scolopaceus.* Abundant migrant in the western part of Manitoba.

66. **Stilt Sandpiper.** *Micropalama himantopus.* On August 29, at Carberry, I made the first positive capture of this species in the Province. It was in a mixed flock of Sandpipers of several species.

67. **Knot, Robin Snipe** *Tringa canutus.* Occasional migrant; noted along Red River and west of Brandon.

68. **Pectoral Sandpiper.** *Pisobia maculata.* A common migrant; noted along Red River.

69. **White-rumped Sandpiper.** *Pisobia fuscicollis.* Migrant; sometimes common, chiefly in western Manitoba.

70. **Baird Sandpiper.** *Pisobia bairdi.* Common migrant, chiefly in Angust.

71. **Least Sandpiper.** *Pisobia minutilla.* A common migrant in all the western part of the Province, especially during August.

72. **Red-backed Sandpiper, Blackheart.** *Pelidna alpina sakhalina.* Reported a common migrant along Red River (*Hine*) and at Portage la Prairie in fall (*Nash*). I have not seen a Manitoba specimen.

73. **Semipalmated Sandpiper.** *Ereunetes pusillus.* Generally distributed as a migrant; especially abundant in the country west of Red River.

74. **Sanderling.** *Calidris lucophaea.* Common migrant; recorded from Lake Winnipeg, Lake Manitoba, Portage la Prairie and Oak Lake.

75. **Marbled Godwit.** *Limosa fedoa.* Summer resident, frequenting the wet prairies near Winnipeg and on the plains of the Souris, etc. Formerly common, now becoming rare.

76. **Hudsonian Godwit.** *Limosa haemastica.* A rare migrant, chiefly along Red River and westward.

77. **Greater Yellow-legs.** *Totanus melanoleucus.* Abun-

dant migrant. Spring migration, late in April; fall, early in August.

78. **Yellow-legs.** *Totanus flavipes.* Abundant migrant in mid-May and in August.

79. **Solitary Sandpiper.** *Helodromas solitarius.* Common migrant, especially in fall; probably also it breeds.

80. **Western Willet.** *Catoptrophorus semipalmatus inornatus.* Common summer resident on all the wet prairies of south-western Manitoba.

81. **Bartramian Sandpiper, Prairie Plover.** *Bartramia longicauda.* In early days this was an extremely abundant summer resident on all the prairies of the Province. It has now become very scarce. Arrives May 7; departs August 30.

82. **Spotted Sandpiper.** *Actitis macularia.* Common summer resident. Arrives May 1, departing late in September.

83. **Long-billed Curlew.** *Numenius americanus.* Summer resident on the wet prairies of the Red River and on the Souris. Formerly common about Lake Manitoba, now rare.

84. **Black-bellied Plover.** *Squatarola squatarola.* Rare spring migrant; no autumn records.

85. **American Golden Plover.** *Charadrius dominicus.* Common spring and fall migrant. Affects burnt prairies and ploughed land. Spring migration, middle of May; fall, in August and September.

86. **Killdeer.** *Oxyechus vociferus.* Common summer resident throughout the Province. Arrives late in April; departs last of August.

87. **Semipalmated Plover, Ring-plover.** *Aegialitis semipalmata.* Rare migrant.

88. **Belted Piping Plover.** *Aegialitis meloda.* Some-

what common, migrant throughout the Province,
and, according to Macoun, found actually breeding
on Lakes Manitoba and Winnipeg.

89. **Turnstone.** *Arenaria interpres morinella.* A rare
migrant. Goes north about May 15; returns about
August 15.

90. **Spruce Grouse.** *Canachites canadensis.* Common
permanent resident of all the Canadian or north-
eastern half of the Province.

91. **Canadian Ruffed Grouse.** *Bonasa umbellus togata.*
Common permanent resident of the Canadian portion of Manitoba.

91a. **Gray Ruffed Grouse.** *Bonasa umbellus umbel-
loides.* Abundant resident of the Alleghanian or
south-western half of the country whereon there is
woods.

92. **Willow Ptarmigan.** *Lagopus lagopus.* A common
resident of the extreme northern parts of Manitoba,
moving southward in winter as far as Shell River,
Lake Manitoba and Shoal Lake.

93. **Prairie-hen.** *Tympanuchus americanus.* In 1871
Dr. Coues wrote: "I have no reason to believe that
it occurs at all in North-western Minnesota or
Northern Dakota." In 1882, when first I visited
Manitoba, the species was nearly unknown in the
country, the only known specimen having been
taken near Winnipeg in 1881. In 1883 W. R. Hine,
informs me, it began to be common at Pembina.
In 1884 it was not only common at Winnipeg, but
had also for the first time made its appearance at
Portage la Prairie, on the Assiniboine. In 1886 I
first saw it at Carberry. Since then it has spread
with cultivation, and is now abundant in all the
settled parts.

94. **Columbian Sharp-tailled Grouse, Prairie Chicken.**
Pediocaetes phasianellus columbianus. Abundant
resident everywhere, especially in the country west
of Lake Winnipeg. north to the narrows of Lake
Winnipeg, and thence eastward as far as Long
Lake and Pic River, on Lake Winnipeg (*Bell*).
This species lives by preference on the prairies in
summer and in the wooded districts during winter,
so that it is in a sense migratory.

95. **Passenger Pigeon.** *Ectopistes migratorius.* In 1885
I wrote as follows: "Common summer resident,
· probably everywhere, as it was noted on Riding
Mountain, along the Assiniboine, on Big Plain, on
Turtle Mountain (*Coues*) and northward, as well
as all over the Red River Valley. throughout the
Winnipegosis region. Often abundant during the
migrations. I am not aware of the existence of any
extensive 'rookeries.' Arrives early in May; departs in October."

In 1908 my notes on the species are: "The following are all the specimens I know of in Manitoba:—
Adult male taken at Winnipeg in 1892, now in collection of Father Blain, St. Boniface College; adult
male taken at Winnipeg in 1894 by E. Wilson, now
in possession of J. K. Hardy of St. Boniface; adult
male taken at Winnipegosis on 13 April, 1898, by
J. J. G. Rosser."

The last year in which the Pigeons came to Manitoba in force was 1878. Next year they were com-
paratively scarce, and each year they have becoms
more so. In the early eighties a few were seen each
season. The above three specimens were the late
reliable recorded. None have been seen since. It
is interesting to note that 1878 was also the last year
of the vast Buffalo herds on the Saskatchewan. In
my collection are three specimens of Passenger

Pigeon: young male taken at Carberry, Man., by
Miller Christy, 30 Aug.,1883; adult male and female
taken at Fort Holmes, Ind. T., U.S., by C. Dewar,
Jan. 1889.

96. **Mourning Dove.** *Zenaidura macroura carolinensis.*
Formerly far from common, now abundant in all
parts of the Alleghanian region where there is
timber, frequenting barnyards that are near the
woods.

97. **Turkey Vulture.** *Cathartes aura septentrionalis.*
Common summer resident of the prairie region,
probably breeding here.

98. **Swallow-tailed Kite.** *Elanoides forficatus.* Geo.
Grieve tells me that two have been taken at Winnipeg, one in 1889 and one in 1892, neither seen by
me. I observed one in Minnesota, near Pembina, in
1883. Coues reports it as occasional at Pembina,
and R. H. Hunter writes me that he has seen it at
Selkirk, Pembina Mountain, and Fort Qu'Appelle.

99. **Harrier.** *Circus hudsonius.* Abundant summer
resident. The adults, in blue plumage, are common
in spring and fall. Arrives April 15; departs
October 15.

100. **Sharp-shinned Hawk.** *Accipiter velox.* Common
summer resident in all wooded regions. Arrives
April 15; departs October 15.

101. **Cooper Hawk or Chicken Hawk.** *Accipiter cooperi.*
May be entered as a rare summer resident. Reported by Hine and Hunter. I saw one at Edmon-
ton, but do not know of a specimen taken in the
Province.

102. **American Goshawk.** *Astur atricapillus.* Common
fall and winter visitor, usually appearing in
August. Not noted during the breeding season.

103. **Red-tailed Hawk.** *Buteo borealis.* Common summer resident of the wooded regions. Apparently complementary of the Swainson Hawk, which is found in more open country and on the prairie. Arrives April 15; departs October 15.

103a. **Krider Hawk.** *Buteo borealis krideri.* Three specimens of this beautiful Hawk have been taken at Winnipeg--one shot at Rosenfeld by Charles Stewart, Sept. 20, 1905; two now in the collection of A. Calder.

104. **Red-shouldered Hawk.** *Buteo lineatus.* R. H. Hunter writes me that he found this species in Eastern Manitoba.

105. **Swainson Hawk. Common Henhawk** *Buteo swainsoni.* Very abundant summer resident of the prairie region; breeds perhaps twice each season. Have seen several black specimens. Arrives April 15; departs October 15.

106. **Broad-winged Hawk.** *Buteo platypterus.* Regular summer visitant wherever there is woods. In my collection are two specimens, one collected near Winnipeg May 3, 19 05, by Ashley Hine. It is reported from various arts of the Province where well timbered, and generally distributed, though not abundant. A. Calder has a beautiful n elanistic specimen, killed at Winnipeg, April, 1907.

107. **American Rough-legged Hawk.** *Archibuteo lagopus sancti-johannis.* Migrant; only seen in spring and fall, but not numerous.

108. **Red Roughleg, Gopher-hawk.** *Archibuteo ferrugineus.* One in the collection of E. W. Darbey was shot, in 1895, at Niverville, fifteen miles south-west of Winnipeg, by Geo. Grieve. There is another specimen in the Manitoba Museum.

109. **Golden Eagle.** *Aquila chrysaetos.* Rare, but apparently resident.

110. **Bald Eagle.** *Haliæetus leucocephalus.* Summer visitant, of general distribution wherever there are fish.

111. **G-ay Gyrfalcon.** *Falco rusticolus.* A rare winter visitant. A specimen was killed near Winnipeg in the fall of 1904, and mounted by E. W. Darbey for the Manitoba Museum. Two fine specimens taken by W. R. Hine were at one time in the same collection.

112. **Duck Hawk.** *Falco peregrinus anatum.* Much like the Goshawk in movements and distribution. Probably breeds in the neighborhood of the large lakes. Quite common on the Big Plain about August.

113. **Pigeon Hawk.** *Falco columbarius.* Common spring and fall migrant, breeding in the woods of northern Manitoba.

113a. **Richardson Merlin.** *Falco columbarius richardsoni.* A Plains race, said to be a regular summer resident along Souris River. A fine specimen was killed in Winnipeg during the summer of 1900 and brought in the flesh to A Calder, in whose collection it may now be seen.

114. **American Sparrow-hawk.** *Falco sparverius.* Abundant summer resident; of general distribution wherever there is woods.

115. **American Osprey.** *Pandion haliaetus carolinensis.* A summer resident about all the fish-stocked rivers and lakes. Reported from all parts of the Province, but rare.

116. **American Long-eared Owl.** *Asio wilsonianus.* Sum-

mer resident in all wooded sections. Arrives April 15; departs October 20.

117. **Short-eared Owl, Marsh-owl.** *Asio flammeus.* Common summer resident in all marshy and prairie sections. Arrives April 1; departs October 30.

118. **Barred Owl.** *Strix varia.* Summer resident of the wooded sections. The records show it to be more widely differed than was once believed. In 1886 I saw a specimen taken at Kenora. In my collection is one taken at Winnipeg, March 30, 1906, by Harry Jones. E. W. Darbey writes me that he had four, taken at Winnipeg in 1906, and one early in April, 1908. At Portage la Prairie I was shown a female taken by G. E. Atkinson, May 19, 1899. J. S. Charleson writes me that on May 9, 1901, while canoeing up the Assiniboine near Winnipeg, he saw a Barred Owl in a tree. Also he secured a specimen from Riding Mountain in January, 1905; it was killed by T. S. Kittson, and had in its stomach a flying squirrel. Arrives about April 1; departs about November 1.

119. **Great Gray Owl.** *Scotiaptex nebulosa.* One specimen, taken on the Big Plain, September 29, 1884. Rather common along the Red River, and resident in the woods about Lake Winnipeg.

120. **Richardson Owl.** *Glaux funerea richardsoni.* A common winter visitant in the Alleghanian region, but probably resident and breeding in the Canadian part of the Province.

121. **Saw-whet Owl.** *Glaux acadica.* Rare, but apparently a permanent resident.

122. **Western Horned Owl.** *Bubo virginianus pallescens.* Common resident wherever there is woods.

122a. **White Horned Owl.** *Bubo virginianus subarcticus.*

Rare in Manitoba; in A. Calder's collection are two superb specimens of this northern form. They were taken recently at Winnipeg. It is recorded also from MacDonald, Duck Mountain, and Touchwood Hills.

123. **Snowy Owl, White Owl.** *Nyctea nyctea.* Common winter visitant, sometimes appearing in large numbers. Arrives October 1; departs April 15.

124. **American Hawk-owl.** *Surnia ulula caparoch.* Very abundant some years. Arrives late in September, and remains until April. May yet be found breeding in the extreme north of the Province.

125. **Burrowing Owl.** *Speotyto cunicularia hypogaea.* There is one of the species that have appeared in Manitoba recently. In the early eighties it was quite unknown.

In August, 1899, at the taxidermist shop of G. E. Atkinson, Portage la Prairie, I saw two Burrowing Owls that were taken by a farmer about four miles north-west of the town, on June 2, 1897. Two others were brought to the shop in May, 1899. The specimen in my collection (No. 2,594) is one of two taken at Morden by D. Nicholson, the taxidermist. He reports it rare, but regular and increasing. Two others were taken in 1902. E. W. Darbey tells me that it is becoming quite common along the Pipestone and on the slope of Riding Mountain.

In 1904 J. P. Turner found a nest eight miles north-west of Winnipeg. The species utilizes the burrows of the Richardson ground-squirrel for a nesting place.

126. **Black-billed Cuckoo.** *Coccyzus erythrophthalmus.* A common summer resident in all the Alleghanian region, not yet recorded beyond that limit. Arrives late in May, departing at the end of August.

127. **Belted Kingfisher.** *Ceryle alcyon.* Common summer resident everywhere along streams and fish frequented lakes. Arrives April 20; departs in October.

128. **Northern Hairy Woodpecker.** *Dryobates villosus leucomelas.* Common resident of woods everywhere.

129. **Downy Woodpecker.** *Dryobates pubescens medianus.* Common resident throughout the Province, excepting possibly the north-eastern corner.

130. **Arctic Three-toed Woodpecker.** *Picoides arcticus.* Common resident in the forested region. Most plentiful in winter, therefore probably in some degree migratory.

131. **American Three-toed Woodpecker.** *Picoides americanus.* Rare permanent resident of the Canadian region. Unfortunately no specimens are available. Both W. R. Hine and R. H. Hunter claim to have seen it in the woods east of Winnipeg, and at Kenora, in 1886, I saw a supposed specimen, beside which its known range includes the forested portion of the Province.

132. **Yellow-bellied Sapsucker.** *Sphyrapicus varius.* Common summer resident of all the Alleghanian region; not yet recorded from the Canadian. Arrives about May 1.

133. **Pileated Woodpecker, Cock-of-the-Woods.** *Phloeotomus pileatus abieticola.* Rare resident in heavy timber and spruce woods throughout the Province.

134. **Red-headed Woodpecker.** *Melanerpes erythrocephalus.* A rare summer resident of south-western Manitoba, apparently confined to regions where oaks are found.

135. **Flicker, Highholder.** *Colaptes auurats luteus.* Very

abundant summer resident throughout the Province wherever there are trees. Arrives April 15; departs September 30.

136. **Red-shafted Flicker.** *Colaptes cafer collaris.* A full plumaged female in my collection (No. 2,546) was shot near Winnipeg, Sept. 30, 1904, by T. Dolphin. At Portage la Prairie, in August, 1899, I saw in G. E. Atkinson's taxidermist shop a fine adult hybrid Flicker, shot in the vicinity, April 16, 1897.

137. **Whip-poor-will.** *Antrostomus vociferus.* Abundant summer resident in woods and partly wooded regions throughout the Province.

138. **Night-hawk.** *Chordeiles virginiauns.* The Nighthawk is common throughout Manitoba, and thus the typical form seems to be the one in all but the true prairie region.

138a. **Western Night-hawk.** *Chordeiles virginianus henryi.* Very abundant summer resident of the prairies in south-western Manitoba. Arrives May 24; departs August 30.

139. **Chimney Swift.** *Chaetura pelagica.* Summer resident of the Alleghanian region, nowhere very common, and most numerous about the towns. Arrives about May 15; departs early in September.

140. **Ruby-throated Hummingbird.** *Trochilus colubris.* This is a summer resident in the Alleghanian region, wherever it finds suitable surroundings—that is, a warm sheltered garden with red flowers. Arriving about May 23.

141. **Scissor-tailed Flycatcher.** *Muscivora forficata.* Accidental straggler. One found by C. W. Nash, at Portage la Prairie, October 31, 1884. (See Auk, April, 1885, p. 218.)

142. **Kingbird.** *Tyrannus tyrannus.* Very abundant

summer resident throughout the Province wherever there are trees or even small bushes. Arrives May 20; departs August 30.

143. **Arkansas Kingbird.** *Tyrannus verticalis.* Two specimens of this, an adult and one in first plumage, were taken by D. Lush Thorpe at the Souris coal fi 's, August 20, 1891. This is not many miles to the .vest of the Province, and justifies the insertion of the species as *probably* Manitoban.

144. **Crested Flycatcher.** *Myiarchus crinitus.* Summer resident about Winnipeg; noted several times at Carberry. Taken by Professor Macoun at Lake Manitoba, June 17, 1881. Quite common along the Assiniboine. On Aug. 20, 1904, I got one at Lake Winnipegosis. This is the northernmost that I know of.

14... **Phoebe.** *Sayornis phoebe.* Rare summer resident, but apparently found in all parts of the Province; recorded even from Norway House.

146. **Olive-sided Flycatcher.** *Nuttallornis borealis.* A common summer resident in all the wooded parts of the Province.

147. **Wood Pewee.** *Myiochanes virens.* Summer resident of the heavy woods in the Alleghanian region.

148. **Western Wood Pewee.** *Myiochanes richardsoni.* Common summer resident of the willow thicket and open groves throughout the Alleghanian region.

149. **Yellow-bellied Flycatcher.** *Empidonax flaviventris.* Summer resident, frequenting woodlands. Noted at Winnipeg, Portage la Prairie, Duck Mountain, and Oak Lake. Probably throughout the Alleghanian region.

150. **Alder Flycatcher.** *Empidonax trailli alnorum.* Recorded from Pembina, Carberry, Lake Manitoba,

Duck Mountain, Riding Mountain, and Norway House, so doubtless it is generally distributed throughout the Province wherever there is cover. An abundant summer resident.

151. **Least Flycatcher.** *Empidonax minimus.* Very abundant summer in all wooded localities. Arrives May 20; departs late in September.

152. **Prairie Horned Lark.** *Otocoris alpestris praticola.* Abundant, breeding in all the · prairie regions. Resident, excepting during December, January, and February. Breeds twice each season.

152a. **Shore Lark.** *Otocoris alpestris.* Fall migrant. Taken at Carberry and Kenora.

153. **American Magpie.** *Pica hudsonia.* Irregular, rare resident. Found west of Fort Ellice, and occasionally along the Upper Assiniboine. A single specimen reported from Brandon.

154. **Blue Jay.** *Cyanocitta cristata.* Common summer resident of woodlands throughout the Province. Arrives early in April; departs late in November. May be resident in southern localities.

155. **Canada Jay, Whiskey-jack. Wis-ka-tjan,** *Perisoreus canadensis.* Abundant resident throughou. the wooded region. The common name of this bird is a corruption of the Indian Wis-ka-tjan. This last name should not be lost sight of.

156. **American Raven.** *Corvus corax principalis.* Winter visitant in all the Alleghanian region. Said to be resident, and of course breeding, in the Canadian regions to the north; not common anywhere.

157. **American Crow.** *Corvus brachyrhynchos.* Summer resident throughout the Province. Abundant in the Alleghanian region: scarce in the Canadian.

158. **Bobolink.** *Dolichonyx oryzivorus.* Abundant summer resident in all the prairie region. Arrives May 20, departs September 7.

159. **Cowbird.** *Molothrus ater.* Very abundant summer resident throughout the prairie region. Arrives May 15; departs 'te in the fall, but disappears for a time during t ; moult at the end of August. They are then to be found, I believe, in the sloughs and marshes with the Grackles.

160. **Yellow-headed Blackbird.** *Xanthocephalus xanthocephalus.* A summer resident of the marshes throughout the Alleghanian region; found also, but much less numerously, in the Canadian region; wherever there are extensive marshes. Arrives May 1, departs late in October.

161. **Northern Redwing.** *Agelaius phoeniceus arctolegus.* Abundant summer resident of the whole Province. Arrives April 20; departs late in October.

162. **Western Meadow Lark.** *Sturnella neglecta.* Abundant summer resident of all the prairie regions. Arrives April 15; departs October 15.

163. **Orchard Oriole.** *Icterus spurius.* One specimen, taken at Pembina, June 6, 1873, by Dr. Coues.

164. **Baltimore Oriole.** *Icterus gaibula.* Abundant summer resident of the Alleghanian region. Arrives May 30; departs August 30.

165. **Rusty Blackbird.** *Euphagus carolinus.* Extremely abundant migrant during April and late September. Not found in the Alleghanian region during summer, but probably breeding in the north-west parts of the Province within the Canadian.

166. **Brewer Blackbird, Satin Bird.** *Euphagus cyanocephalus.* Abundant summer resident, apparently

confined to the Alleguanian region. Arrives April
15; departs November 1.

167. **Bronzed Grackle.** *Quiscalus quiscula aeneus.*
Abundant summer resident wherever there is woodland. Arrives April 20, departs October 15.

168. **Evening Grosbeak.** *Hesperiphona vespertina.* Com-
mon winter visitant in the vicinities of Winnipeg,
Portage la Prairie, and Qu'Appelle, Big Island in
Lake Winnipeg, and Selkirk. (*R. H. Hunter.*)

169. **Pine Grosbeak.** *Pinicola enucleator leucura.* Common winter visitant in all the wooded sections,
probably breeding in the northmost parts of the
Province.

Purple Finch. *Carpodacus purpureus.* Common
summer resident of all wooded regions. Arrives
early in May; departs middle of September.

171. **English Sparrow.** *Passer domesticus.* This species
is now found in all the settled portions of Manitoba,
and at every farmhouse and in all the towns of the
North-west as far as Athabaska Landing, Alberta,
about N. Latitude 55, W. Longitude 113. It first
appeared at Carberry in 1892, but was not found in
numbers until 1894. According to Criddle, it is
developing a habit of migration.

172. **American Crossbill.** *Loxia curvirostra minor.* Common as a winter visitant at Winnipeg, Portage la
Prairie and Big Plain, possibly breeding, as it is
known to do so in Minnesota (*Trippe*).

173. **White-winged Crossbill.** *Loxia leucoptera.* Common winter visitant about Winnipeg and Big Plain;
may breed in the Canadian region.

174. **Gray-crowned Finch, Pink Snowbird.** *Leucosticte
tephrocotis.* I have in my collection an adult of
species taken near Birtle, Manitoba, in January,

1891, by George Copeland. Also in the Manitoba Muse·m are two specimens taken in the Province by W P. Hine These give a considerable eastward extension to the range of the species.

175. **Hoary Redpoll.** *Acanthis hornemanni exilipes.* Noted only as a rare migrant; in fall and winter accompanies *A. linaria.*

176. **Redpoll.** *Acanthis linaria.* Abundant fall and winter visitant, arriving from the north about October 20, and departing about May 1.

177. **American Goldfinch.** *Astragalinus tristis.* Common summer resident of the Alleghanian region. Arrives last week of May; departs middle of September.

178. **Pine Siskin.** *Spinus pinus.* An irregular and abundant spring and fall visitant; may breed in the Canadian region.

179. **Snowflake, Snow-bunting.** *Plectrophenax nivalis.* Very abundant spring, fall, and winter resident, arriving about the middle of October and staying until the end of April.

180. **Lapland Longspur.** *Calcarius lapponicus.* Very abundant spring and fall migrant. Arrives May 15, and again September 20.

181. **Painted Longspur.** *Calcarius pictus.* Abundant spring and much less plentiful fall migrant. Arrives on May 10, stays two weeks, and again on September 15 for a few days.

182. **Black-breasted Longspur.** *Calcarius ornatus.* Common summer resident of the dry prairies. Local in distribution, many pairs sometimes affecting a limited area of dry prairie, while again for miles no more of the species are to be seen. Arrives May 16; departs August 30.

183. **McCown Longspur.** *Rhynchophanes mccowni.* A

specimen of this bird, taken by D. Losh Thorpe, near Dalesbro, just west of our borders, justifies its inclusion as a probable straggler.

184. **Western Vesper-sparrow.** *Pooecetes gramineus confinis.* Very abundant summer resident of the prairie region. Arrives May 1; departs September 30.

185. **Savanna Sparrow.** *Passerculus sandwichensis savanna.* Doubtless found as a summer resident in open places throughout our Canadian area, as Preble found it general in Keewatin and at Norway House.

185a. **Western Savanna-sparrow.** *Passerculus sandwichensis alaudinus.* Abundant summer resident of the prairie region. Arrives May 1; departs September 30.

186. **Baird Sparrow.** *Coturniculus bairdi.* Abundant summer resident throughout the prairie region wherever there are alkaline flats. Taken at Grand Rapids (*Nutting*).

187. **Leconte Sparrow.** *Ammodramus lecontei.* Abundant summer resident of willow bottom-lands throughout the prairie region. Arrives May 1; departs September 30.

189. **Nelson Sparrow.** *Ammodramus nelsoni.* In 1892 I found this sparrow abundant at Carberry and secured specimens, both breeding and migrant. In 1901 I found it common at Shoal Lake. In my collection are three specimens taken at Winnipeg. There can be little doubt that it is found throughout south-western Manitoba, and breeds wherever found.

189. **Lark Sparrow.** *Chondestes grammacus.* Rare summer resident. Noted only in the vicinity of Winnipeg and at Portage la Prairie.

190. **Black-faced or Harris Sparrow.** *Zonotrichia querula.* Abundant spring and fall migrant. Arrives May 15 and again September 20, remaining a week or ten days each time. Breeds in Hudsonian fauna. Nest found in far north. See Auk, Jan. 1998, p. 72.

191. **White-crowned Sparrow.** *Zonotrichia leucophrys.* Migrant, not common. Passes through in early May and late September. Probably breeds in the extreme north-eastern part of the Province.

191a. **Gambel Sparrow.** *Zonotrichia leucophrys gambeli.* A migrant only, abundant on the Souris in fall migration (*Coues*). I have seen specimens taken at Carberry and at Portage la Prairie.

192. **White-throated Sparrow.** *Zonotrichia albicollis.* Common summer resident of all the wooded country Arrives early in May; departs late in October.

193. **Tree-sparrow.** *Spizella monticola.* Abundant migra. . all parts of the Province from mid-April to n. . .ay, and again through October.

194. **Chipping Sparrow.** *Spizella passerina.* Summer resident about small towns and along wooded edges, apparently throughout the Province, as it is recorded from Pembina, Winnipeg, Norway House, Oxford House, Grand Rapids, Prince Albert, and Qu'Appelle, as well as Carberry and Portage la Prairie. Not common; mid-April to late September.

195. **Clay-colored Sparrow.** *Spizella pallida.* Very abundant summer resident of the Alleghanian region. Arrives May 15; departs October 1.

196. **Slate-colored Junco.** *Junco hyemalis.* Abundant migrant throughout the Province, and doubtless breeding in all the Canadian region, though there are few records of it. Arrives the first week of April, and departs in October.

197. **Montana Junco.** *Junco hyemalis montanus.* Among the migrant flocks of the preceding I have several times seen this race near Carberry ; one or two were collected.

198. **Song Sparrow.** *Melospiza melodia.* Summer resident throughout the Province. Not common. Arrives late in April; departs early in October.

199. **Lincoln Sparrow.** *Melos, .. lincolni.* Spring and fall migrant. Noted during 1st week of May and last week of September. Probably breeding in the extreme north-eastern part of the Province.

200. **Swamp Sparrow.** *Melospiza georgiana.* Common summer resident throughout the Province, but most abundant in the Alleghanian region.

201. **Fox Sparrow.** *Passerella iliaca.* Common migrant in the prairie region, arriving in mid-April. Breeding abundantly on Duck Mountain and apparently in all the Canadian region of the Province.

202. **Townee.** *Pipilo erythropthalmus.* Common summer resident of the Alleghanian region north at least to Carberry; not yet recorded beyond.

203. **Arctic Towhee.** *Pipilo maculatus arcticus.* This Western species appears in this list on the strength of a specimen taken on the Souris at the boundary, September 16, 1873, by Dr. Elliot Coues.

204. **Rose-breasted Grosbeak.** *Zamelodia ludoviciana.* Common summer resident of the Alleghanian region, possibly farther, as there is one record for the north end of Lake Winnipeg.

205. **Indigo Bunting.** *Passerina cyanea.* A male adult Indigo Bunting (No. 2,531 Seton Coll.) was killed on June 3, 1893, by W. R. Hine, near St. Boniface, between the Seine and Assiniboine Rivers, on the

land between the Bishops's Marsh and the River Seine. Another adult male was taken at Estevan, South Saskatchewan, by D. L. Thorpe, 29 May, 1892. Estevan is eighty miles west of Manitoba. In the collection of Father Blain, St. Boniface College, is an extraordinary specimen killed at Winnipeg. After careful examination E. A. Preble and I agree that it is probably a hybrid Indigo Bunting X Common Canary, maybe escaped from captivity. With the general form and color of an Indigo Bunting female, it has some patches of yellow, and a white tail and wings.

206. **Dickcissel or Black-throated Bunting.** *Spiza americana.* August 10, 1899, I was shown an adult specimen of this bird by G. E. Atkinson, who shot it at Portage la Prairie, June 1 , 1897. This was recorded in "Man. Free Press," March 5, 1901.

207. **Scarlet Tanager.** *Piranga erythromelas.* I have seen two specimens that were taken at Winnipeg in 1892, one in the collection of George Grieve, the other in the collection of W. R. Hine. He also took another, and saw a third in 1888. It was about the end of May, during a sudden cold spell. The third he saw on the bank of Red River in the city limits; he was within two yards of it for some time, but did not collect it.

R. H. Hunter writes me that in June, 1880, while camping east of Winnipeg, he observed a pair, evidently nesting, and adds that his companion, Clementi-Smith, has "seen several pairs on the shores of Lake Winnipeg." "Lake Winnipeg" (*Ridgway*). "Rare at Qu'Appelle" (*Guernsey*).

208. **Purple Martin.** *Progne subis.* Common summer resident of all the Alleghanian region wherever there is large timber to furnish nesting sites; also in towns.

209. **Cliff Swallow.** *Petrochelidon lunifrons.* Abundant summer resident in all parts of the Province where cliffs or tall buildings in quiet places furnish nesting sites. Arrives May 15; departs August 30.

210. **Barn Swallow.** *Hirundo erythrogastra.* A summer resident of erratic distribution. Seldom seen about Winnipeg, not recorded from Portage la Prairie, and yet in 1904 J. S. Charleson the taxidermist told me it was common at MacDonald and at Brandon. There is quite a colony at the former place under the long bridge. At Carberry I saw one or two each year; they arrived in the first half of May. Thus there are many records to show that, though rare, it is of general distribution, and further, it is increasing with the advance of settlement. Near Wawanesa, on September 13, 1904, I saw a long straggling flock of nearly a hundred of the species flying south-west; many were within three or four feet of me as I drove.

211. **Tree Swallow.** *Tridoprocne bicolor.* Abundant summer resident in all parts of the Province where there are large trees.

212. **Bank Swallow, Sand Martin.** *Riparia riparia.* Common summer resident wherever it can find suitable banks for nesting. Arrives mid-May; departs late in August.

213. **Saw-winged Swallow.** *Stelgidopteryx serripennis.* In the Manitoba Museum is a specimen of this Swallow, taken at Winnipeg by W. R. Hine.

214. **Bohemian Wax-wing.** *Bombycilla garrula.* A common winter visitant in most parts of Manitoba; often seen in November and April. Not known to nest here.

215. **Cedar Wax-wing, Cherry Bird.** *Bombycilla cedro-*

rum. Abundant summer resident throughout the Province. Arrives late in May.

216. **Northern Shrike.** *Lanius borealis.* Common spring and fall visitant, passing through toward the north in the first half of April, returning during October.

217. **White-rumped Shrike.** *Lanius ludovicianus excubitorides.* Abundant summer resident throughout the Alleghanian regions. Arrives early in May; departs late in September.

218. **Red-eyed Vireo.** *Vireosylva olivacea.* Abundant summer resident wherever there is cover in all parts of the Province. Arrives May 24; departs late in August.

219. **Philadelphia Vireo.** *Vireosylva philadelphica.* A regular summer resident, not abundant, but probably in the woodlands throughout the Province. I found the nest and eggs near Fort Pelly (north-west of Duck Mountain), June 9, 1884. (See Auk, July, 1885, pp. 305, 306.)

220. **Warbling Vireo.** *Vireosylva gilva.* Common summer resident of the Alleghanian region. Arrives May 30.

221. **Yellow-throated Vireo.** *Lanivireo flavifrons.* This species has not yet been taken in Manitoba, so far as I know, but being an Eastern species taken at Yorktown, Sask., by W. Raine, and at Moosejaw by Miller Christy, it is included as probable. W. R. Hine claims to have seen it on the Red River.

222. **Blue-headed Vireo.** *Lanivireo solitarius.* Summer resident in all parts of Manitoba; not common. Arrives about May 15.

223. **Black and White Warbler.** *Mniotilta varia.* Summer resident in all the wooded parts of the Province;

apparently most numerous in the spruce forests of the Canadian region. Arrives about May 15; departs at the end of August.

224. **Nashville Warbler.** *Helminthophila rubricapilla.* Rare summer resident. Noted at Aweme, Lake Manitoba, Duck Mountain, and along Red River.

225. **Orange-crowned Warbler.** *Helminthophila celata.* Common summer resident of all woodlands, apparently throughout the Province. Arrives May 12; departs end of September.

226. **Tennessee Warbler.** *Helminthophila peregrina.* Summer resident, breeding in most woodlands, but not plentiful. Noted on Big Plain and Duck Mountain, and along Red River near Winnipeg. At Pembina common in the spring migration (*Coues*). North shore of Lake Winnipeg (*Kennicott*). Aweme (*Criddle*). Arrives in mid-May; departs at the end of September.

227. **Cape May Warbler.** *Dendroica tigrina.* Abundant migrant along Red River and a common summer resident in some regions, but erratic in distribution. Recorded from Winnipeg, Shoal Lake, and Moose Factory. Migrates in mid-May and late August.

228. **Yellow Warbler.** *Dendroica aestiva.* Very abundant summer resident of all thickets and woods throughout the Province. Arrives May 15; departs September 7.

229. **Myrtle Warbler.** *Dendroica coronata.* Abundant migrant throughout the Province, breeding in the Canadian region. Arrives April 23; departs September 12.

230. **Magnolia Warbler.** *Dendroica magnolia.* Noted only as a migrant, but doubtless breeds in the Canadian region. Arrives mid-May; departs early September.

231. **Chestnut-sided Warbler.** *Dendroica pennsylvanica.* Common summer resident in woodlands of the Alleghanian region. Arrives about May 20.

232. **Bay-breasted Warbler.** *Dendroica castanea.* A regular migrant, especially along Red River; not common. Probably breeds in the northernmost part of the Province. Arrives mid-May.

233. **Black-poll Warbler.** *Dendroica striata.* Noted only as a migrant; not plentiful. Arrives at Aweme about May 13.

234. **Black-throated Green Warbler.** *Dendroica virens.* Norman Criddle reports this at Aweme on May 13 and 17, 1898.

235. **Blackburnian Warbler.** *Dendroica blackburniae.* A rare migrant in the Alleghanian region, probably breeding in the Canadian. Arrives late May.

236. **Pine Warbler.** *Dendroica vigorsi.* A rare summer resident in the evergreen forests of South-eastern Manitoba. "Arrives about May 10; departs about September 2" (*Criddle*).

237. **Palm Warbler.** *Dendroica palmarum.* A common spring and fall migrant in the Alleghanian region; may breed in the Canadian. Passes about the first week of May, and again about September 15.

238. **Ovenbird.** *Seiurus aurocapillus.* Common summer resident of woodlands; apparently found throughout the Province. Arrives in mid-May; departs in mid-September.

239. **Water-thrush.** *Seiurus noveboracensis notabilis.* Common summer resident of all woodlands where there is water. Arrives in mid-May; departs late in September.

240. **Connecticut Warbler.** *Oporornis agilis.* Somewhat common summer resident from mid-May to early

September. Noted on Duck Mountain, Big Plain, and along Red River. Nest found June 21, 1883. (See Auk, April, 1884, pp. 192, 193.)

241. **Mourning Warbler.** *Oporornis philadelphia.* Common summer resident of dry scrub lands throughout the Alleghanian region, arriving in late May, "departing early in September" (*Criddle*).

242. **Northern Yellowthroat.** *Geothylpis trichas.* Common summer resident of thickets in the Alleghanian region, arriving about May 20, departing in September.

343. **Wilson Warbler.** *Wilsonia pusilla.* Summer resident throughout the Province; not common. Arriving in mid-May, departing in mid-September.

244. **Canadian Warbler.** *Wilsonia canadensis.* Apparently found throughout the Province as a rare summer resident. According to N. Criddle it arrives about May 20 and departs the last of August.

245. **American Redstart.** *Setophaga ruticilla.* Common summer resident of all woodlands Arrives in mid-May; departs in mid-September.

246. **American Pipit.** *Anthus rubecens.* Abundant spring and fall migrant throughout the Province.

247. **Sprague Pipit., Missouri Skylark** *Anthus spraguei.* Formerly resident summer of Assiniboine region wherever there were high dry prairies, arriving May 1, departing September 1. This bird was very abundant on the Big Plain in 1882, but in 1892 I failed to see or hear a single individual in the country. It appears to have totally disappeared. This is unquestionably owing to the breaking up of the virgin prairie.

248. **Catbird.** *Dumetella carolinensis.* Abundant sum-

mer resident of the Alleghanian region. Arrives in mid-May; departs mid-September.

249. **Brown Thrasher.** *Toxostoma rufum.* Common summer resident of the Alleghanian region wherever there are open woodlands. Arrives May 15; departs September 7.

250. **Western House Wren.** *Troglodytes aedon parkmani.* Abundant summer resident, apparently confined to the Alleghanian region. Arrives May 20; departs about the end of September.

251. **Winter Wren.** *Nannus hiemalis.* This is a woodland species, apparently common in the southeastern quarter of the Povince only. R. H. Hunter found it a common summer resident in the woods east of Winnipeg. C. W. Nash saw one at Winnipeg, and another at Portage la Prairie. N. Criddle found it at Aweme.

252. **Short-billed Marsh-wren.** *Cistothorus stellaris.* Summer resident of the Alleghanian region; erratic in distribution. Preble found it at Norway House. Arrives May 15; departs Sept. 15.

253. **Long-billed Marsh-wren.** *Telmatodytes palustris iliacus.* Summer resident; of extensive, though erratic, distribution. Common at Winnipeg, Shoal Lake, and Portage la Prairie. Recorded at Oak Point, Aweme, Waterhen River, and on Saskatchewan. Arrives early in May

254. **Brown Creeper.** *Certhia familiaris americana.* A rare summer resident. Noted at Winnipeg and Portage la Prairie, and Riding Mountain.

255. **Slender-billed Nuthatch.** *Sitta carolinensis aculeata.* Somewhat rare resident of the heavily timbered regions. Absent from the Province only during the hardest part of the winter.

256. **Red-breasted Nuthatch.** *Sitta canadensis.* Rare summer resident of the woods in all parts of the Province; abundant during the migration in September.

257. **Long-tailed Chickadee.** *Penthestes atricapillus septentrionalis.* Resident; abundant in all the woodlands. The Manitoba bird is not strictly *septentrionalis,* but is nearer to that form than to *atric.;pillus.*

258. **Hudsonian Chickadee.** *Penthestes hudsonicus.* The only record is as follows:—"In flocks around the Porcupine Mountains" (*Macoun*). The bird is certainly not found in the Assiniboine region, and there are no Red River records, though it should be the prevailing species in the Winnipeg Basin.

259. **Golden-crowned Kinglet.** *Regulus satrapa.* Rare migrant. Noted at Carberry, November 5, 1884, and recorded also from Aweme, Portage la Prairie, and Winnipeg.

260. **Ruby-crowned Kinglet.** *Regulus calendula.* Common migrant. Noted on Big Plain about May 15, along Red River, and at Portage la Prairie. "On Souris in September" (*Coues*). Probably breeds in the north-east part of the Province. Passes through in late April and early May; again about the 1st of October.

261. **Willow Veery.** *Hylocichla fuscescens salicicola.* Abundant summer resident of all thickets in the Alleghanian region. Arrives in mid-May; departs early in September.

262. **Gray-cheeked Thrush.** *Hylocichla aliciae.* Common migrant. Imperfectly observed. as it is not usually distinguished from the next.

263. **Olive-backed Thrush.** *Hylocichla ustulata swainsoni.* Common summer resident of woodlands

apparently throughout the Province. Arrives May 1; departs early in October.

264. **Hermit Thrush.** *Hylocichla guttata pallasi.* Common summer resident of woodlands in the Canadian region. A migrant in the Alleghanian, passing in late April and early October.

265. **American Robin.** *Planesticus migratorius.* Abundant summer resident throughout the Province. Arrives April 15; departs October 15.

266. **Bluebird.** *Sialia sialis.* Formerly very rare; has become quite a regular summer resident in the country along the Assiniboine, and nearly every grove of oak of any extent is found to have a pair making their home in it along with the Purple Martins.

268. **Mountain Bluebird.** *Sialia currucoides.* E. H. Patterson secured one of a pair that he found at a place two miles west of Brandon, and sent the same to G. E. Atkinson, who recorded it in "Man. Free Press," March 5, 1904. To this, Norman Criddle (the naturalist responsible for records from Aweme) adds ("Ottawa Naturalist," July, 1904, pp 85, 86) that the species is by no means uncommon about the Carberry sandhills, and that he has taken numerous nests there.